©Copyrighted 2019, Collette Owens Dishman

All rights reserved.

No part of this publication may be reproduced or transmitted in any form or by any means, electronic or mechanical, including photocopy recording, or any information storage and retrieval system without permission in writing from the publisher.

ISBN: 978-1-948638-59-3

Published by

Fideli Publishing, Inc.
119 W. Morgan St.
Martinsville, IN 46151

www.FideliPublishing.com

PRINTED IN THE UNITED STATES OF AMERICA

About the Author

Collette Owens Dishman is a native of Cookeville, Tennessee and now resides in Livingston, Tennessee with her husband of twenty-three years, Ronald. She is the daughter of the late Clarence W. and Clena (Flatt) Owens. The granddaughter of the late Porter and Rachel (Thornton) Owens and the late Ermon B. and Lola Brady (West) Flatt.

Collette attends Fredonia Community Church in Livingston where she is presently the Teen/Young Adult Sunday School Teacher and serves as Church Clerk.

"I didn't accept my Lord and Savior until my early thirties and never dreamed of the journey that I now travel. I wouldn't trade the journey I have been on for anything as I have grown so much as a person and as a Christian. God has been so good and wonderful to me and I just praise Him for His many blessings."

Collette accepted her Lord and Savior in February of 1989 and was baptized on Easter morning of March 1989. She soon saw the evidence of God working in her life, but it wasn't until 1994 that she began noticing words were staying in her head, mind, heart, and soul. She started writing them down getting a thought or theme from a sermon, a hymn, a testimony, God's creation, a trial, a blessing, or an answered prayer. Late in 2015, she started thinking of putting her words in a book and started compiling her poems into a book format but was interrupted with a decline in her health. Doing much better and getting stronger with each new day, the finished project is what you now hold in your hand.

My goal for this book is that it will help encourage, uplift, strengthen, comfort, heal, or just draw someone to the Lord. Wouldn't that be wonderful?

My prayer and hope is that you will be blessed by these words as I am through this journey we call life. Happy reading and may you hear His whisper. God bless you and your family.

Collette Owens Dishman

Table of Contents

Do It Again 1
Precious Savior, Blessed Jesus 2
His Garden of Love 5
His Loving Compassion 7
The Wonder of His Will 9
He Loves You 11
The True Right Way 13
Somebody's Watching 15
The Celebration 17
A Small Step of Faith 19
Stretch Forth In Prayer 21
Over the Blood of Jesus 23
The Invitation 25
One Decision — The Only Way 27
An Airway of Blessing 28
The Ultimate Sacrifice 31
Our Christmas Tree 32
An Oasis of Hope 35
In The Palm Of His Hand 36
The Birthday Man 39
Waiting For The Rain 41
The Old Time Shepherd 42
Crocheted Prayer Cloth 46
Through a Daughter's Eyes 47
Crosses in the Sky 51
The Blanket of Prayer 53
The Light in the Valley 55
The Journey of Twenty-Ten (2010) 57

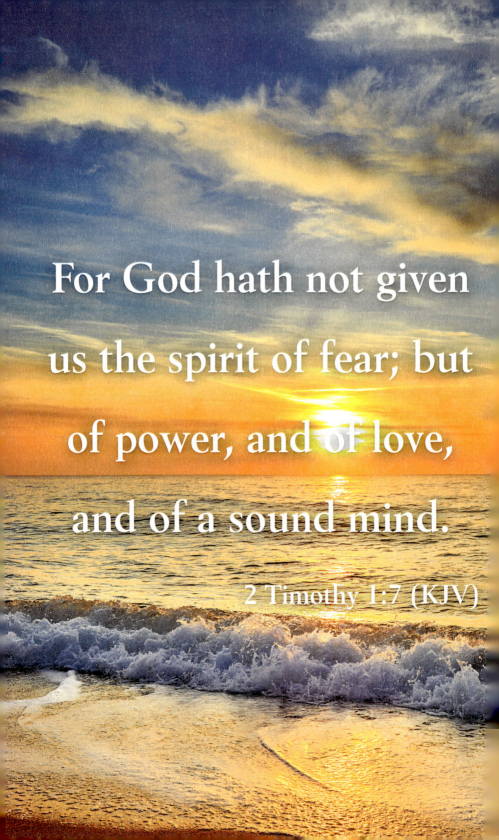

Do It Again

When life gets you down
Put a smile on your face
And do it again
Jump back on your feet
And join the human race
And do it again.

Just do it again
Do it again
You can't give up
Be a "trifling pup"
Forget all the rest
And do your very best
Just do it again.

November 1994

Precious Savior, Blessed Jesus

(The following words came to me as I was driving down Hwy. 111 one day — when I was desperately trying not to get down. I started singing these words to keep my spirits up.)

>When your down and all discouraged
>Never fear nor never fret
>Place your trust in One who loves you
>You will have no regrets.

CHORUS:
>Precious Savior, Blessed Jesus
>He's your Leader and Your Guide
>Precious Savior, Blessed Jesus
>He will give eternal life.

>When your hurt and feel alone
>And you think nobody cares
>Just think of Whom you belong
>Just remember, He's everywhere.

When your heart is overflowing
Then your cup is very full
A precious Savior and Dear Friend
At your heart strings He will pull.

The saving plan is very simple
All you do is believe and ask
For Him to come into your heart
And you'll have peace and joy at last.

Now our time is close at hand
And His coming is very soon
Simply believe, obey, and trust Him
And escape eternal doom.

June 4, 2001

His Garden of Love

February is known as the month of love,
For old and young alike.
All we need to do is look above,
And feel His wonderous light.

Acts of love always in motion,
For those in despair and need.
But God's love is the potion,
All we have to do is plant the seed.

February 9, 2002

His Loving Compassion

Today hurt, disease, and grief is the fashion,
We pray and long for Jesus' powerful touch.
Moved by His unconditional and loving compassion,
We praise and thank Him very much.

February 2, 2003

The Wonder of His Will

I stand amazed and awe in wonder
From where I came and where I'm going
To a heavenly home high up yonder
No more burdens I'll be towing.

Even in His presence of trust and care
Feelings of doubt, unworthiness and fear
Turning me from my true friend — if I dare
But quietly He said, "Child I am here."

Now I know the Lord God's love is true
His promises He never breaks
To do His will is the clue
Believing, willing, praying, praising — is all that it takes.

November 22, 2003

He Loves You

Jesus loves you,
And so do I.
I'll be praying for you,
Both day and night.

Have you made your choice,
Please friend don't delay.
Place your trust in Jesus,
And be saved today.

Freedom from pain and strife,
No more tear-stained eyes.
Blessings so overflowing,
In your new eternal life.

June 14, 2004

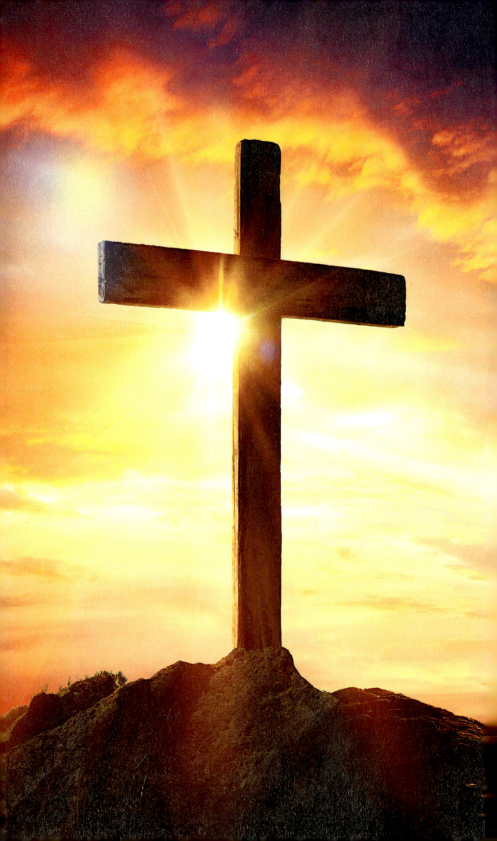

The True Right Way

Based on Proverbs 14:12

Blessings of God upon you,
Never to be taken away.
Look to His word for the clue,
And enjoy His peace and blessings today.

Find the good way of the Lord,
By seeking the right path.
To ignore this warning, you can't afford,
Seek Him now and avoid His wrath.

Forget the cares of this old world,
Don't build up your treasures here.
Salvation awaits for every boy and girl,
Eternal life with Jesus awaits us without fear.

Worry about what's in the church house,
From these things don't depart.
Let others hear your joyful shouts,
Jesus lives within my heart!

August 8, 2004

Somebody's Watching

Child arise call upon God
Be brought down to your knees
Awake, don't sleep nor nod
Be a light and witness to all who sees.

Be careful of your speech and thoughts
Don't think you can run or hide
Satan will make you doubt by your faults
But through Jesus we know the devil lies.

Don't think no one sees or cares
Be careful of the faith you choose
Kill, steal, and destroy if you dare
Somebody's watching, eventually you'll lose.

Jesus our Savior sees and knows all
Didn't come for our sins to chastise
Upon His glorious name you can call
Above all, mercy and love will rise.

August 29, 2004

The Celebration

Dearest Family and Friends,
My time on earth is now done
Please don't weep or fret
I'm going to meet God and His Son
With arms wide open and a paid sin debt.

Today is a time to celebrate
No time for sadness or tears
Blessings, rewards, and joys await
A long-awaited homecoming is near.

Loved ones gone home before me
Will be waiting upon my arrival
Loving faces longing to see
Oh, what a heavenly revival!

Oh, loved one, today don't delay
Accept Jesus in your heart
Eternal life and happiness is His way
From His presence we'll not depart.

Jesus loves each of you
And has a purpose for your life
Sharing this message is the clue
Let it be said you fought the good fight.

The Celebration (CONTINUED)

Never give up and never doubt
Make the right choice now
Songs of praises we need to shout
And all before Him we'll humbly bow.

When Jesus is all that you have
He will supply all your needs
We know not the day nor the hour
Seek His forgiveness down on your knees.

Remember this is a celebration
Rejoice in His great light
I'm claiming His promise in Revelation
To my mansion I go in my heavenly flight.

September 7, 2004

A Small Step of Faith

It's only a small step
No more room for hate
Be drawn, deny thyself
And step out in simple faith.

He's longing to be near you
And be ruler; now Master and Savior
Accepting Him is long overdue
Accept His grace — God's blessed favor.

All good gifts come from above
In my place, He obediently stood
Pure, unconditional love
Just for you and me He would.

January 20, 2007

Faith is having the courage to let *God* have control.

Stretch Forth In Prayer

Inspired by Bro. Junior Foster's Sermon on Feb. 28, 2007

Now when you're down and out
And your burdened with a load of cares
Never fear nor never doubt
Just stretch forth in prayer.

When uncertainty is looming all around
Reluctantly we feel life is unfair
Don't let that devil get you down
Just stretch forth in prayer.

When you've obediently served awhile
Always desiring to do more if you dare
Go and take that extra mile
By just stretching forth in prayer.

Sinner you know your lost and undone
And your looking for that peace and joy so rare
Believe, trust, confess in God's only Son
Seek and accept Him by stretching forth in prayer.

March 1, 2007

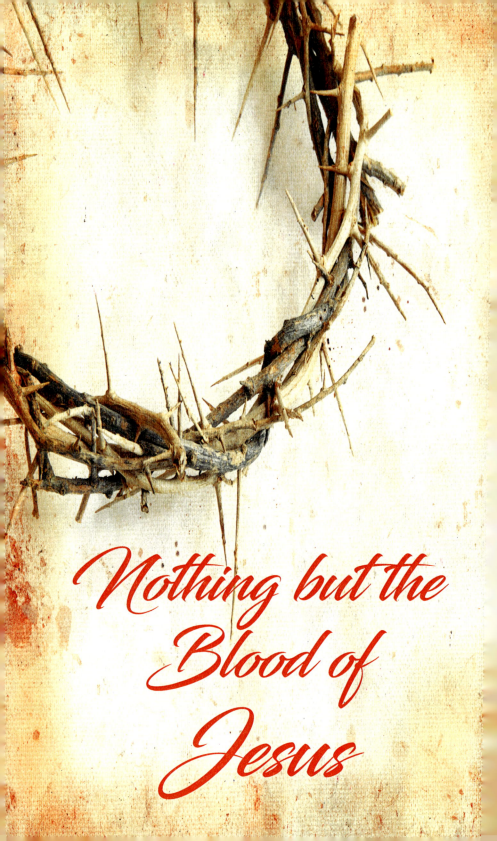

Over the Blood of Jesus

Over the blood of Jesus
And over our heap of prayers
Oh, sinner that's going to hell
We're making it hard for you to go there.

It's easy, it's simple you see
By faith through our Lord Jesus
Crucified, died, buried, and risen
All this for you and for me.

We're fighting the good fight
With each fresh and new day
To keep you from your gloomy flight
Through Jesus' blood is the only true way.

June 22, 2007

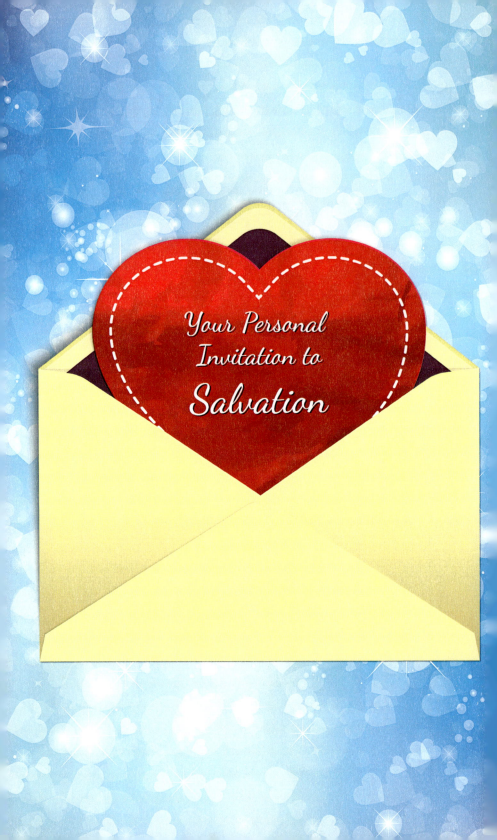

The Invitation

Dear Friend,

You're invited to receive a wonderful gift
Accept it, take it, get a joyous lift
God said, "Come to me ... and I will give you rest."
Choose salvation, eternal life, and enjoy God's very best!

What will you do with God's invitation?
Please choose to be part of Heaven's celebration
At morning, noon, and evening sunsets
Our sins, God not only forgives them, He forgets.

August 28, 2007

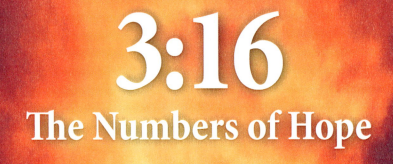

One Decision — The Only Way

Dear Friend,

The only decision you need to make
The free gift of grace from God — yours to take
Salvation, not religion, is so simple
Love, peace, joy spreads as a wave's ripple.

Simple faith and trust are all you need
God's Holy Word of Truth you must read
Jesus died, was buried, and rose on the third day
Believe this truth through the blood of Him —
Jesus is the only way.

Call out to our precious Lord and Savior
Let others see your new kind of behavior
Ask Him into your heart — calling on His name
Eternal life with Jesus will feel like a refreshing summer rain.

November 6, 2007

An Airway of Blessing

*(Written For Bro. David Carr and
Staff of King of Kings Radio Network)*

One dedicated man of God
Planted one tiny precious seed
Began an airway of love and blessings
Available just for you and for me.

Good folk with testimonies and life-filled stories
With hearts of brokenness and hearts of pure joy
Just looking for that tiny ray of hope
Messages in songs played, they find they can cope.

Discouraged by the worldly affairs
Not knowing who to believe
Your King of Kings family really do care
By bringing the truth in love for us to see.

Waves of love, hope, peace, encouragement, and Good News
Sent through the ministry of a special brother,
sisters, and others too
They'll tell you With The Help of the Lord
We Stand in the Gap and
With Zeal We Proclaim The Wonderful Word of God
Broadcasting twenty-four seven by the
simple grace of our Father God.

Sending out the awakening alarm
On daily important issues
Changing lives, one song, one testimony at a time
Through Helping Hands and Shareathon
our listeners are so very kind.

October 13 - 16, 2008

The Ultimate Sacrifice

I wrote the following for the Memorial/Fountain Dedication on the Livingston, TN Courthouse Square and In Memory of Brad McCormick and Jeremiah Savage Memorial on Terrorism:

They Gave the Ultimate for Our Freedom

They willingly took their place
In the war against terrorism
Young heroes and humble Americans
Each a team player showing no favoritism.

Messages of understanding and peace to be heard and to be had
We were so loved by these proud and defending lads
Nothing was too great or too small
With their lives they paid it all.

Today we are here to thank, honor, and respect
To show our gratefulness, remember, and do not forget
That our freedoms are never really free
Brad and Jeremiah gave the ultimate sacrifice for you and for me.

So dear neighbors and dear friends
Don't let their sacrifice be in vain
Spread their mission of peace and love and make amends
And do it all in Jesus' name.

August 22, 2009

Our Christmas Tree

This time of year and all around
The air is filled with excitement and celebrations
Greetings of love and joy spreads across town
Yards and homes adorned with different decorations.

Our house is not excluded from all this glee
The house is filled with the smells of this joyous season
A variety of ornaments bring life to our Christmas tree
And now I will explain each of their reason.

Our tree holds round shiny decorative ornaments
That is God's unconditional and circle of love that never ends
For in those difficult times and trying moments
For all - His help and direction He does send.

The dove is the peace found in a life in complete submission
The manger scene is the first Christmas and the One true gift
Red and green bows tells of God's gift to us — simple salvation
To celebrate on a day set aside — December twenty-fifth.

The candy stripes and candy canes
Is His sweet mercy and sweet grace
Shown to us at the cross and through His pain
For us He shed His blood and took our place.

The snowflake like the new fallen snow
Pure and white — our new robe will be we are told
A cluster of gold grapes is known as our fruits of the spirit
Peace, love, joy, goodness, and all others to merit.

A jingle bell rings "to jingle with joy for Jesus"
Sounding out the glorious Good News
The church house where brothers and sisters are united with us
Singing His praises galore flowing from each pew.

Proverbs 3:5 reminds us of WHO to completely trust
And in Him alone we certainly must
Keeping a loved one's memory alive is a homemade ornament
Twinkling clear lights completes our tree's adornment
For Jesus is the light of the world
He came to seek and save every boy and girl.

Yes, this is our Christmas tree
Trimmed in red, green, silver, and gold
Its branches are filled with much love and a plea
To believe and accept the greatest story ever told.

December 20, 2010

An Oasis of Hope

Sickness, evil, struggles and trials
Enduring and fighting hard to try to cope
Face them head on with your smiles
Turn to Jesus — your Oasis of Hope.
Three steps forward and two steps back
There are days you feel you're at the end of your rope
Plenty of joy, love, and strength you'll not lack
When you turn to Jesus — your Oasis of Hope.

2011

In The Palm of His Hand

(This poem is based on the Sunday School Lesson and Morning Worship Message by Bro. Eric Beaty and Bro. Jerry Harris from the following passages of God's Word — Ephesians 6:10-18; 1 John 5:4; Matthew 11:28-30; James 5:11 (KJV); and given to me by the Holy Spirit. Thank You Jesus!)

Life is full of contention, struggles, surprises, and strife
Wrestling to keep our relationship pure with God;
oh my, what a fight
Holding on to all of the strength that you can
Reach for the power in the palm of His hand.

Sickness, pain, grief, depression, and fear
Becomes more apparent with each passing year
But just learn of Him — receive His instruction —
it's all part of His plan
And reach for the power in the palm of His hand.

The Rock — our Lord Jesus Christ — we must place our faith in
Be patient, persevere, continue to endure to the end
His promise to us — against all evil when we take a stand
Victory is ours
when we reach for the power in the palm of His hand.

So my dear friend be of good cheer
The coming of our precious Savior is drawing near
Be watchful, be aware, become part of the Heavenly band
When you reach for the power in the palm of His hand.

Be sure you are ready from this world to go
Our dear Savior, Jesus, loves you so
One drop of blood He did shed for whosoever across this land
It's the source of power in the palm of His hand.

June 10, 2012

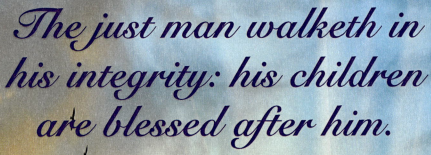

The just man walketh in his integrity: his children are blessed after him.

~ Proverbs 20:7 (KJV)

The Birthday Man

*(This was written for Bro. David Carr
of King of Kings Radio Network, Somerset, KY on his birthday)*

A man named David living each day the best he can
His ministry proclaiming the Good News 24/7 all across the land
Today is his special day and if you can
Send your best wishes to the birthday man.

This brother is never afraid to take a stand
Against the issues in God's Word you can scan
Lying, drinking, drugs, and man with man
Heed the warnings from the birthday man.

When one is in need, he offers a helping hand
So now it's our turn
To do something grand
Let us be a blessing to the birthday man.

November 13, 2012

Waiting For The Rain

Beaten, discouraged, and so very tired
So bravely battling unspeakable pain
"How much longer Lord?" you inquired
He said, "You have to be waiting for the rain."

So many daily struggles and trials
Seem their presence more stronger daily gain
With faith and hope you endured the difficult miles
Persevere and just keep waiting for the rain.

It seems your being attacked from each and every side
Everything you do and every step you take seems lame
Just trust in Jesus, He is your Savior and Guide
And remember your waiting for the rain.

Your soul has been renewed, refreshed, and restored
When your answer and blessings from prayer finally came
The praise and gratitude from your humble heart outpoured
Because obediently you were waiting for the rain.

March 11, 2013

The Old Time Shepherd

(Bro. Jerry Harris)

On a June day in 1940 on a mountain called Highland
This old time shepherd's journey truly began
The seventh of ten children born to Luther and Belle
Jerry was named out of his brother's primary reader;
an interesting tidbit to tell.

The old time shepherd to be didn't attend school very much
To get out of going he volunteered to wash dishes,
sweep, mop, and such
A favorite teacher, Ms. Beulah Smith,
made his days interesting and bright
But still this old time shepherd never learn to read or write.

Prayers were sent up to the Lord by Jerry's mother, Belle
Her heart's desire for her family;
the Lord would call one to be a preacher

The Lord heard and abundantly answered
her special request without fail
Two sons, one grandson, two great grandsons —
all called to be preachers.

This old time shepherd left his mountain home
as is so often a part of life
He moved up north and met a pretty young girl
that would soon become his wife
Jerry Harris and Mary Ruth Adams were married in June of 1965
He thought she was the prettiest thing; mercy sakes alive
They lived in an Indiana apartment on a street name Pearl
Along came Mary Katherine (known as Kathy);
their precious little girl.

After the old time shepherd
moved back to his mountain home in 1968
In the spring of that year a very important decision Jerry did make
At a revival meeting at the fairgrounds where it would all start
This old time shepherd to Jesus Christ he gave his heart.

Jerry listened to the words of Bro. Livingston; lovingly known as
Bro. Norm
Sending out the Good News; again you must be born
Thirty-five years ago, this old time shepherd's journey did begin
His first dismissal prayer at Highland was "Oh Lord, Amen!"

Bro. Jerry (at Highland) served as deacon
with Bro. Loren and Bro. Donald
These three faithfully served the Lord and their church;
oh, what models

They were respectfully called Peter,
James, and John over the years
Often from the woods their fervent prayers
would reach the community's ears.

A different plan the Lord now had for our Bro. Jerry
As a called preacher the Good News he wanted him to carry
Excuses kept going through his mind,
telling him he can't and leaving him faint
Seeking relief and an answer
he sought the advice of a dear old saint.

To Florence he did confide his uncertainty of his calling to preach
She showed him how to get the Holy Ghost
to work for him and let it teach
She said, "Tell them you 'think' the Lord has called you to preach"
And this will be your way out if your calling isn't reached.

On a Thursday night in 1978 behind the pulpit
from where he stands
Announced his calling and began reading God's Word
with the leading of the Spirit's hand
The answer was now very clear
and in God he put his complete trust
Bro. Jerry accepted his calling to preach and just knew he must.

To make his ministry more effective, genuine, and sound
This old time shepherd patterned his style of preaching
after Bro. Melvin Brown
When the time came to leave his beloved mountain home church
His letter, after several attempts to write it,
was stained with the tears of Sis. Faye, the clerk.

Throughout all the years of his ministry many faithful men and
women of God helped Bro. Jerry get his start
They encouraged, led, and guided Bro. Jerry
to a true shepherd's heart
A shepherd's work is a humble work and his sheep know his voice
To bring life and love of God to the lost;
this is his desire and his choice.

Today we have set aside to show you our love,
thanks, and appreciation
We are so blessed by your genuine love, prayers,
and gentle direction
Your life is not your own and many miracles
and blessings are still to be shared
For now we are praising the Lord for this old time shepherd's
unselfish help and care.

October 27, 2013

Crocheted Prayer Cloth

(I wrote this note/poem to go along with prayer cloths that I had crocheted)

Dear Friend,

This little prayer cloth
Was made especially just for you
Lovingly bathed in sweet prayer
Asking God's blessings on you.

Your need I ask His will to meet
For in Him no problem is too deep
Come boldly to God's throne where help is found
Courage, strength, comfort, healing, peace abound.

So, when you feel alone, down, and out
Remember He is with you — don't you doubt
Just remember this prayer from this blessed cloth
Have faith, believe, trust as Jesus taught.

August 11, 2014

Through a Daughter's Eyes

The hardest thing I had to do at the ripe old age of nine
Was to learn to share my daddy and his heart with many others
But believing and trusting I knew everything
would work out and be fine
Because in Christ they were all our neighbors,
sisters, and brothers.

Through the years we've met lots of people
who helped us with their special touch
We'd grown to love them but soon had to say our goodbyes
Each time we left, daddy would always say,
"You'll love the next ones just as much"
That's a shepherd's and daddy's love and encouragement seen
through a daughter's eyes.

It breaks my heart whenever you boldly stand
Behind that old pulpit and preach your heart out.
Always being led by the Holy Spirit's hand
You gave the warning,
and some refused to listen and were full of doubt.

Because of the love for my daddy and pastor
all I want to do is protect him
In my fleshly self, frustration, hurt, and anger start to rise
Remembering God's promise that He is always by your side;
you're in His care,
He loves you — these emotions start to dim
Because that's the ultimate protection
seen through a daughter's eyes.

I see a man who gives so freely of himself, his family, and time
As you stand each Sunday against the devil's lies
Keeping future problems from affecting the church
by staying in the true vine
This is a true shepherd of the flock seen through a daughter's eyes.

Standing behind the pulpit and never ashamed
to tell people you couldn't read
Thirty-seven years later the swelling pride
of your daughter still thrives
Standing there knowing you couldn't preach unless the
"Preacher came and help plant the seed"
Through your obedience miracles happened in our family
as seen through a daughter's eyes.

I knew how many sleepless nights
and how many times he knelt to pray
Just because a precious soul crossed his mind
"Lord, I'll be willing to give my blessing to someone else,"
I heard him say
So that person could make it a little farther —
this shepherd's love is so kind.

Words can never tell you how proud I am to be the preacher's kid
First, always, and forever you'll be my daddy and then my pastor
Praising God for blessing me with you as He so lovingly did
What a true gift from my Heavenly Master.

To fill your shoes when someday I grow up and my heart sings
The life lessons you taught me anointed as one so wise
You will always be the wind beneath my wings
This is the story of my daddy and pastor
as seen through a daughter's eyes.

October 2, 2014

Crosses in the Sky

Sickness, worries, troubles, and trials
Many times leave me only to sigh
Constantly rebuking the devil and his wiles
A reminder I'm not alone are the crosses in the sky.

Lined out against a backdrop of clear blue
Straight white fluffy tails left from jets and planes to fly
Proclaiming His love as if on cue
His message sent from the crosses in the sky.

When I am anxious, sad, and low
All I have to do to get by
Bringing sweet peace to my weary soul
Is look up and see the crosses in the sky.

Three white crosses all in a perfect row
One Easter morn up above proudly stood high
Over death, hell, and the devil, the foe
Victory! Proclaimed the crosses in the sky.

When down in the valley with the daily woes
There's assurance God's love is always nigh
Seeking His grace, mercy, strength — knowing one place to go
Just look to the heavens for the crosses in the sky.

May 22, 2016

The Blanket of Prayer

(Written While I Was a Resident in the Overton County Nursing Home & Health Rehab Center)

In each of our lives the unexpected arises
It's overwhelming and seems more than we can bear.
Anxiety, stress, worries, uncertainties rises
Trust Him and wrap these in the blanket of prayer.

Not knowing what lies ahead
He said we would always be in His care.
Rest in His peace, love, and power
And cover yourself in the blanket of prayer.

When the body is sick and weak
And the weakness, time, and routine begin to wear
Seek His power, strength, and healing
With the Master's blanket of prayer.

Encouraging and comforting each other as we can
We all have trials and troubles we share
In the spirit of one mind, one accord in unity
We're taken care of in the blanket of prayer.

July 2, 2017

The Light in the Valley

When your depressed, discouraged, and down in the valley
And you try to hold on with all your might
Just reach for that wonderful light in the valley
And let its strength and warmth help your spirit be quiet.

Some journeys are like going down a deep dark alley
Wondering which direction to go is going to be right
Oh so grateful for that light in the valley
It's there to dispel the darkness of the night.

In trials and troubles we all must together rally
And hold onto our Savior's promise oh so tight
Our weapon the beautiful light in the valley
May it always shine bold and bright.

August 20, 2017

The Journey of Twenty-Ten (2010)

I was just going along life's way,
But that all changed on a cold February day.
With joy trying to serve my Savior,
I was sick, but God still showed me His favor.
Lessons of balance, trust, faith, obedience He did send,
On my new journey of twenty-ten.

The Lord had, for me, other plans and a new direction,
By His grace and mercy He showed me His loving correction.
Child you need to take care and slow down
And for you see the next wonderful blessing ever to be found.
Yes, lessons of balance, trust, faith, obedience He did send,
On my new journey of twenty-ten.

Knowing in my spirit a change was coming
From it, I knew I shouldn't think about running.
A still small voice lovingly came in the night,
Whispering, child, your going to be alright.
I knew I needed the knowledge and help of a doctor's skill
So I completely submitted to my Savior's will.
Not knowing where, how, why, or when,
Humbly I went on my journey of twenty-ten.

Being not anxious, worried, or scared,
I knew God wouldn't give me more than I could bear.
Unknown what was waiting around the bend,
By faith I continued my journey of twenty-ten.

Oh I am so glad I let God have His own way,
The blessings and miracles were many that February day.
Everywhere I looked I seen the evidence of God's mighty touch,
With each breath, I praised and thanked Him so very much.
Lessons of balance, trust, faith, obedience He did send,
Through this - my journey of twenty-ten.

A brotherly friendship strengthened; a God-sent surgeon,
Family and friends' well wishes and prayers-they were merging.
A sister became a sister-in-Christ with others soon to follow,
Pity, fear, depression - in them I knew I could not wallow.
In a few short weeks I was rapidly on the mend,
Praising my Lord every day on my journey of twenty-ten.

Each new day brought unexpected blessings fair,
Showering and blessing me with their love and care.
I would look forward to seeing my "angel" nurses,
We prayed and shared our favorite Bible verses.
Balance, trust, faith, obedience He did send
To learn and be shared on the journey of twenty-ten.

Came the news of no weight bearing for six months,
This didn't phase me one bit — some even thought I was nuts.
To some that would seem like forever - but oh not to me,
Not able to do anything — I still had God's best gift you see.
Praying for those in need, a prayer list was born with my ink pen,
Weaken but blessed,
I'm serving God on the journey of twenty-ten.

Now I am almost completely healed,
In my heart God's promises are sealed.
Grateful for each encouraging and good doctor's report,
God's faithfulness is stronger than ever before.
Sharing with family and friends the trust and faith God did send,
That helped me to grow on the journey of twenty-ten.

Now we are in the new year of twenty eleven,
Still keeping my sight on my new home in Heaven.
Many times, to my shame, I still fall short,
Oh to hear
"Well done thou good and faithful servant," God's final report.
I continue this walk praying that Heaven is it's final end,
Because of the lessons learned in the journey of twenty-ten.

January 15, 2011